Chamomile Poems

Peggy Insula

Dedication

For Rosa Baptista,
Our Brevard County, Florida,
Poetry muse,
And for my patient husband,
Eugenio Insula,
And my live-in artist and
technical assistant,
My grandson,
Zander Kelly

Old School Poet

I'm an atavistic poet.
I search for rhyme and beat the
time
Of verses that I can call mine.
I'm not modern, and I know it.

My language is inhibited;
The f-bomb makes me shrink and
cringe.
I guess I'm writing on the fringe
Of modern works exhibited.

There are rules that give us
might
To elucidate in verses clean;
I hope you know what my words
mean
Within the rules I use to write.

Living on the Indian River Lagoon

Unwinding on the River

When I walk through my door,
the river meets me there.
I feel the stress no more
that all day long I bear.

Cares slide off my shoulders;
onto the floor they drop,
No more weight like boulders—
the river whispers, "Stop."

King of the Lagoon

A dolphin broke the water
with its sharp and sturdy fin.
With a start, I gasped out loud
at the majesty of him.

With great confidence he cruised
and left ripples in his wake.
Full of purpose, he swam south
to where foaming sea waves
break.

I wondered if he had come
to find breakfast over here
in our still, gray-green lagoon
where large mullet schools
appear.

His regal mien and his sleek
form
evoked full-blown respect.
Cloaked in harmony, he showed
lack of fear in his aspect.

He had for me a lesson,
of that fact, I'm fairly sure:
to adapt to my surrounds
and to swim with courage pure.

Birdy Benediction

A small white heron stood
upon my window sill
and stared into my room.
At what? I'm wond'ring still.

The day outside was fine:
sun and skies of blue—
no reason to escape
or shelter somewhere new.

My guest met my eye
with fixed and shiny stare.
She didn't even flinch
to see me standing there.

Her feathers glowed so white,
a shining aura formed.
Had she come to warn me
of some approaching storm?

Or had she come to give
a blessing from above—
a pure and radiant sign
of our Savior's love?

She gave me widened eyes
and breathless sense of awe
at her daring presence
in our encounter raw.

She stayed for quite a while
framed in my window's light.
The river flowed beyond
and beckoned her to flight.

She slowly stretched her wings
as she regarded me,
and then she flapped away
and headed for the sea.

Undecided Sky

Today the morning sky
did not know what to do.
Should it stay solemn gray
or turn itself to blue?

It drew a line so fine,
horizontal, and so true:
Above the line was gray,
below, a sky of blue.

And thus, the sky remained
steadfast an hour or two
until the smiling sun
transformed the gray to blue.

A Squirrel at the Lagoon?

The ripples on the river twitched
and flickered in the morning
bright.
A squirrel sat on the white
seawall
and preened his tail—no sign of
fright.

Sunbeams dashed across the
river;
still that squirrel sat on the wall.
Perched on the largest big white
rock,
poised in profile, preening still.
What gall!

There were no nearby trees to
climb
if a predator pursued him.
With no escape, no place to run,
he'd find himself out on a limb.

Yet still he paused beside the
river,
and leisurely he cleaned his face.
To me a light bulb moment
shone:
my patio was his safe place.

Surprising the Baby Mullet

On a cool, bright day,
I lie belly-down
on the planks of the pier.
I scan the surface
of the gray-green water
and search for little fish.

They're not here today.
My heart sinks
toward the lonely lagoon,
but, reviving hope,
I sprinkle cereal nuts
that gently bob
and slowly settle,
easing downward,
out of sight.

Seconds pass;
a skittish school
of finger mullet forms.
How do they know?
They linger, hover,
gather courage,
and with daring darts
they snatch the prizes

and dash back down
into their school
beneath the reach
of any foul fowl
that might interrupt
the pleasure
of their afternoon surprise.

Bon Appetit!

Two little flitter-birds—
who knows what they are? —
skim across the water
in the early morning sun.
Are they searching for
their breakfast fish,
swimming just below?

The surface of the water
Splits predator from prey
By the merest inches:
Birds skim above;
Fish swim beneath
The river's mirror calm.

Sometimes the Lagoon is Placid

Its waters flow so peacefully—
with wrinkled surface not yet
rippled—
I let its calm persistence lull me
till all my senses become tickled.

I'd be energized, but I'm asleep,
in a deep, delicious river doze.
Life doesn't get any better than
this;
as everyone on the river knows.

Am I neglecting all my chores?
I surely am, but I don't care.
The river's siren call is more
beguiling than all riches rare.

So, I'll soak up all its
peacefulness
while it restores my saddened
soul
and refills me with the joyfulness
that mindless living from me
stole.

Hungry Herons

On my patio,
A fisherman stands.
He holds up a fish
that he now lands.

He's just a statue,
but herons are fooled.
Stock still they stare.
Does he offer food?

The birds come as near
as bravery lasts.
They figure it out,
and fly off downcast.

A Winter Morning in Florida

Outside my window,
across the narrow bank,
gray skies drop rain that plops,
dimpling the wide and lively
lagoon.

Five squawking pelicans in a
flock
squabble and splash, stirring up
spray and spume.
They're fighting over fishing
rights
or dominance or mates.

*In flight, they glide, and skim the
surface,
heads hunched back—sure and
sedate.
But diving, they crash headlong
without a trace of grace.*

*Onto the patio I stumble
and glare at the raucous beasts.
"Be quiet out there, rowdy
rascals!
People are trying to sleep."*

Misty Morning

The fog snuggled up
on my patio
and enveloped me
with its moist cloak.

Dense, it hovered there
before the dawn.
I could not see sky
nor birds nor lawn.

I stood enraptured,
comforted, blessed.
Of all forms of weather,
I love fog best.

Serenity

The sun streams through my
window now;
a month of persistent rain is
gone.
And out upon the bright lagoon,
happier times have not been
known.

Tiny whitecaps form and sparkle
on their casual way to shore.
The water's in a mood serene,
inviting me to come outdoors.

To rest and dream on my back
porch
and let mind's current carry me
to mystic places far and wide
on my lagoon ride toward the
sea.

Morning Mystery

The gleam of gold on our lagoon
dazzled my eyes at early dawn
when near the bank my vision
drawn,
I gasped, leaned in, a creature
moved.

A snake-like, black appendage
poised,
then disappeared without a
trace,
only to rise and break the face
of our river, without a noise.

An elephant trunk, I then recalled,
and that led me to realize
that a manatee of baby size
was cruising south by our seawall.

Our river life is still quite rife,
and my great hope is that it stays
stable across the future's haze
of our unfaithful steward strife.

Vanishing Birds

From my aerie on the porch,
I lost a flock of birds today.
They flew above the cold lagoon.
(Air fifty degrees, but bright sun
rising.)

An astonishing show of snow-
glow white—
tiny aviators with angled
wings—
soared and swooped, to
disappear
amongst the gleaming sea-wall
rocks—

The perfect camouflage—maybe
a roost
to catch the rays of morning sun
and warm their night-chilled
bones
at this wall that blocked the
breeze.

When minutes passed and no
bird rose,
I rose myself. Outside, I crept
onto the pier
and scanned the rocks below
to find no birds, nor fluffy down.

Where did they go?
I scratched my head and thought
and thought,
but one thing now was clear:
Birds need no magician to make
them disappear.

Rhythms of Life

Our life-giver kissed the river
and dappled it with dazzling
light.
I stood upright and said goodbye
to the Florida winter night.

My cool and cozy pre-spring
sleep,
lulled by the lap of gentle waves,
gave in to dawn's insistent call
to "rise and shine" and "seize the
day."

Transitions here are ever quick,
from day to night and night to
day.
The laggard will be left behind—
time's onward march will not
delay.

I've prob'ly missed a lot of life
with the slow drag of my feet.
"Quality and not quantity"
is my permission for retreat.

I'm basically a lazy soul;
I love the comfort of the nest.
I only pray that I can find
the bless-ed balance that is best.

A Blue Awakening

I wake up in a dark pit.
Unshed tears weigh down my
heart.
Outside, the sky is gloomy gray.
For the first time ever,
I take an extra crazy pill.
I make a cup of coffee
and sip it on the balcony.
The breeze and the river
are my comforters.
At last, I cry.
A torrent of tears is a blessing,
cleansing my heart,
opening my mind,
easing my pain.

Pain from what?
My husband suffers
the effects of chemotherapy.
I cannot ease it.
A group of friends has dissolved.
Am I the cause?
Unloved as a child, I'm
unlovable now
by most others.
Mostly, I'm okay with that,

but when I risk attachment
and meet with rejection, I hurt.
I remind myself that my
business
is how much I love others
and not whether they love me.

All better now.

Wake Up Call

At dawn, my head still full of
chalk,
I took my doggie for a walk.
A raindrop smacked me on the
head.
"Wake up, you sleepy oaf," it
said.
"We've been working overnight
creating streams for your
delight.
Clear water ripples over grass
And puddles stand where you
stood last.
In your warm and cozy bed,
Did you hear thunder overhead?
Did you feel its trembling roll?
Did its rumble rouse your soul?

Now you're awake and standing there,
water dripping from your hair.
Feel the breeze that strokes your skin.
Embrace the gray clouds creeping in.
Inhale the crisp, clear, cleansing air.
We cleared it for you in our care.
Place yourself within the scene
of this, our marvelous morning dream."

Patio Plant Rebellion

Patio Plant Demands

There's a riot on my patio.
It's growing quite absurd.
All the plants are up in arms,
demanding to be heard.

Water me more often!
Put me in the sun!
I need to be repotted!
My blooming time is done!

Feed me! Fan me! Trim me!
Move me away from him!
Let me climb! Give me a lamp!
The winter light's too dim!

And that dog you put out here,
keep him away from us.
Up till now, he's done no harm,
but we're nervous, cannot trust.

We're getting kind of crowded,
but we like to propagate,
Give us more room at once.
We don't want to wait.

You should sit with us more
often
and sing a soft, sweet tune.
Not that heavy metal,
Crashing drums or big bassoon.

We are tough but tender.
Our sentiments are keen.
But you already know this.
You're our garden queen!

Taming the Cactus

My cactus does not trust me.
Why? I do not know.
All I do is care for it
and pray for it to grow.

I water it and feed it
and turn it toward the sun.
You'd think that it would know
by now
that it and I are one.

Yet every time I'm near it,
it stabs me with a spike—
a tiny spear I can't remove—
Does it know what that feels
like?

Does it think I'm going to eat it
like they do in Mexico?
Served up with a tortilla
and huevos rancheros?

I wish that it would live in peace
and set its fears aside.
I only want to nurture it
without prickles in my hide.

Pouting

My bougainvillea's mad at me,
and this time, I know why.
I moved it back a couple feet,
so workers could get by.

They installed a shutter
to protect it from a storm.
I moved that sullen plant right
back,
but still it changed its form.

In stubbornness, its branches
drooped.
In spite, its leaves grew small.
It snubbed me and would not
respond
to any care at all.

Soft and tenderly, I coaxed it,
and every day I pled.
A season later, I gave up—
I thought that it was dead.

*Then one day I noticed
bright leaves begin to grow
big and lush, low on the branch,
but their growth was slow.*

*How long will this pout go on?
I'm ready for an end.
Sure as rain, that plant must
know
I want to be a friend.*

*I feed it and I water it
and keep its feet wet too,
just the way that it prefers.
What more can I do?*

Please forgive me.

Escape

I have a funny cactus
out on my patio,
and it has lately chosen
an eccentric way to grow.

It clambers up the walls
and hangs on tendrils fine.
Why it doesn't fall—
on this I can't opine.

Where does it think it's going?
Is it trying to escape?
From what? To where? And why?
Should I hold it up with tape?

Understanding slowly dawns.
My cactus must feel blue.
"On gloomy days like this," I say,
"I'll climb the wall with you."

Terror on the Patio

A little tiny lizard
sits on a flower stem.
He thinks that the porch plants
belong exclusively to him.

He flaunts at me his colors
when I come out the door.
He thinks that I'm afraid of him
'cause he's a dinosaur.

I want to give respect
to this ferocious beast,
so I give to him my back
and into the house retreat.

Plant Complaint

I stepped onto the patio
in dread and trepidation,
I had to learn what's going on
in my little garden nation.

"It's cold," they cried
as I stepped outside.
"Bring us some heat,"
the refrain repeats,
"or some of us may die."

"Calm down," I pled.
"You won't be dead.
The winter is not pleasing,
but I'm glad to say
I checked today,
and none of you are freezing."

"Take us into the house;
give us a douse—
warm water on our roots."
"Are you kidding me?
That just can't be.
When I moved you last,
such a pout set in,
I never could win,
and the grumbling never passed.

"My advice to you
is to let it be,
and accept each changing
season.
This too shall pass,
and you will see
your worry's without reason.

"You've lived here now
for many years,
and each of you has grown.
What you need is trust, not
fears.
You'll surely reap what's already
sown."

Each of them regarded me
with doubt formed on their
leaves,
but little by little, their branches
eased,
and small, soft sighs were
heaved.

As they soaked in what I'd said,
they realized their choices:
to accept things without dread
and let peace
bloom upon their faces,
or to damage their roots and
bruise themselves
kicking against the traces.

Rebuttal

Surrounded by plants,
I sit on the porch.
With hands on my knees,
back straight, I lean for'd.

"Listen up, you guys.
This job is hard.
I'm doing my best
to be always on guard

"And meet your needs.
Each of you, unique and rare,
sometimes provokes me
to pull out my hair.

"I read your minds.
For this I am made.
I learn your language
from cactus to jade.

"And yet you puzzle me.
I'm not good enough
To keep each of you happy—
That's really YOUR stuff.

"Make up your minds
to adapt here in peace.
I'm not Mother Nature,
but I'm YOUR mother, at least.

"Let's make the best of it
and give thanks for our
planting.
You won't do any good,
resisting and ranting."

The Penta's Perspective

I poured out my problems to my
penta
    whose red blooms had never
ceased.
    and with my soul unburdened,
    my worries, too, decreased.

"How do you stay so cheerful
    whatever strife life brings?"
    "It's genes and grace and
humility
    in the face of everything."

"How do you find these
attributes?"
    I asked the pretty plant.
    "Why, trust and prayer enable
me
    to do the things I think I can't."

Her sturdy stems and hardy
leaves
    support her scarlet flowers
    that wave gently in the breeze.
    Her courage never cowers.

"You're a model," I say to her,
"an example for us all.
in whatever wind that blows,
we don't have to fall."

"That's right," she said,
and her blooms shone.
"Each day brings a chance for joy
we may have never known.

"And it's enough to seek
for the mystery in each day
and not to question how or why
things turn out this way."

This trusting flower has taught me
confidence in life,
and peace within the tapestry
of happiness and strife.

A Breath of Hope

Those grumbling plants on the
patio
are happy with me today
It's because I fed and watered
them,
and 'cause spring is on its way.

They seem to give me credit for
that,
and I'll hardly turn it down.
They've spent all winter mad at
me,
and smiles are better than
frowns.

I'll gladly trim and pamper them
to stay in their good graces,
I'll tell them stories and sing
them songs
and kiss their flowering faces.

They are the hope of a winter's
end,
and the promise of new growth,
and these things are of exceeding
worth
for green plants and mankind
both.

Patio Poise

There is a flow'ring plant out
here;
she's always cheerful and
sublime.
Her blossoms orange always
appear
in ev'ry season, ev'ry clime.

I look to her to cheer myself
when most all the others whine.
Her fresh flowers give me a
wealth
of comfort warm and hopeful
times.

Her lush green leaves and
sturdy stems
are witnesses of glowing health.
She appreciates her frequent
trims,
and when I'm with her, true love
brims.

She's learned the gift of
gratitude
and blooms where she is planted.
Secrets of life are in her mood,
and happiness is granted.

Mountain Mama Memories

The Walnut Tree's Surprise

Way up on the mountain
when I was ten years old,
we had a walnut tree
that never failed to hold
out branches full and free.

It soared skyward and it spread
its branches far and wide.
Its shade enticed us there
to rest awhile outside
and lay down all our care.

The tree was home to life:
birds and caterpillars
inhabited this tree,
and many walnut stealers
besides my family.

My uncle and I sat
on stumps beneath that tree.
    An apple idly held,
he was regaling me
with lies he liked to tell.

A caterpillar fell
and landed on the fruit.
I held my breath in spite:
this scene could be a hoot.
Right then, he took a bite.

He grimaced, spit, and gagged;
    rolling on the grass I laughed—
The worm, first long and green,
    was now cut clean in half.
    Funniest sight I'd ever seen.

"I know you saw that worm.
Why didn't you tell me?"
My uncle's rage was rife.
I only asked with glee,
  "What does worm taste
like?"

Lost in the Woods

Way up on the mountain
when I was four years old
I took a kindling stick,
laid out my uncle cold.

Sitting on the porch edge,
"I'll kill your dog," he said.
Right then, I sneaked behind
    and whacked him on his head.

He rolled off of the porch
and landed in the grass.
He writhed and moaned and yelped;
    my grandma ran out fast.

With hands upon her hips
she cried, "What have you
done?"
But I was well away.
I told my dog, "Let's run!"

We tore across the fields
and dashed into the woods
through vines and briars
and brush.
Long out of breath, we
stood.

Scratched up and stained
with sweat,
I sat down on a log
and began my vigil
with my beloved dog.

Time crept by in baby steps
while I worried what the cost
of my misdeed would be.
No matter—I was lost.

No one would come for me.
I knew that from the start.
Survival of the fit
lodged in my fam'ly's heart.

I leaned back on my log
and waited for a clue.
No answer came to me;
I knew not what to do.

Twilight crept up on me;
the sun sank in the west.
The dog I had defended
got bored with me and left.

As dusk came on relentless,
a sound that I knew well
came faint and from afar—
the ring of Bessie's bell.

I knew that cow was headed
back to her comfy barn.
If I could only find her,
she'd lead me to the farm.

I slogged my way back
home
by following the cow
Grandma barely noticed;
the heat was over now.

And from that date it seems
that all the teasing stopped.
Good things can sometimes
come
when a bully's head gets
bopped.

*I look back and ponder
how Bessie rescued me.
And if it weren't for her,
still 'neath that tree I'd be.*

*That rotten log would hold
my skeleton upright,
picked clean by careless
crows
indifferent to my plight.*

Aging

Rescued at Sea

Sailing on the twilight river,
and heading out to sea,
I came upon a small leaf-boat
with someone hailing me.
Leaning over the side, I stared
and slowly turned my head.
And then I cupped my ear to
hear
a voice. "Ahoy!" it said.

Large swells surged up to rock my
boat
and the tiny leaf 'long side.
A little figure, one-inch tall,
waved open arms so wide
he nearly swamped his green
leaf-boat.
I caught my breath and said,
"How can I help?"
"Toss me a line," he pled.

And then, that whelp, he
stamped his feet!
   The leaf-vein held him fine.
   I dangled fishing filament;
a rope would never do.
   "Here you are," I called out to
him.
   "And now, it's up to you."
   He grabbed the line in his wee
hand,
   and I held my end tight.

   I scanned waves for a sign of
land,
   but none came into sight.
   "Come right on up," I called to
him,
   "and we can set you free."
"Oh, no," he said. "You've got it wrong.
You're coming down to me."
That's when his grin, his
gleaming eyes,
   entranced me on the spot.

*Against my will, I grabbed the
line.
It quivered and grew hot.
"Ah-ha, this line will never hold,"
I told the little guy.
But then, I shrank, and shrank, and
shrank
beneath the w-i-d-'-n-i-n-g sky.
And down the swaying line I
slid,
a yo-yo on a string.*

*My captor gave his hand to
shake
And said, "Now here's the thing:
I've rescued you. No need to
quake,
And you can call me 'King.'"
Then frantically, I spun around
and sought to find the shore.
"There's no need for you to
worry.
You won't see that anymore.*

"We're on a great adventure,
friend.
Who knows what's now in
store?"
His loving eyes held mine in
trance.
I knew that it was true:
No wild escape was there for me;
I was in for something new.
I lay supine on my leaf-side,
head in hands and ankles
crossed.

Try as I might, I could not feel
that anything was lost.
We two sailed the sparkling
waters,
companions side by side.
We praised the birthing of the
stars
And waited for the tide.
Fears for the future washed
away
in the wake of waters wide.

Aging

I've been dragging my tail for
days,
leaving dust trails of chores not
done.
I go back to bed in the morning
and rise with the setting sun.

Do I have a low-grade infection?
Have I crossed some kind of line?
Is senility setting in?
Is it time for my decline?

Growing old, I thought, was
gradual,
not a sudden, startling plunge—
a faulty elevator dropping,
shocking me to grasp and lunge.

No time to orient myself,
become accustomed to the shift.
I'm on a downhill drop, not slide,
and it's for sure I need a lift.

Should I have myself cremated
or be plopped into a hole?
This decision for the end of life
looms larger as a goal.

The church frowns on cremation;
my husband says, "Hell, yes!"
Should I just die and let my folks
figure out this mortal mess?

The Address Book

As I searched through my
address book—
made thirty years ago, it read,
I turned a page in search of you.
"That woman there is dead," I
said.

I held my breath and turned a
page—
more traces shown of folks now
passed.
Some were friends; some family,
acquaintances that didn't last.

By the end, in my hand I held
a heavy tome of time gone by,
filled with folks now flown
away—
I never thought that they might
die.

My list for Christmas cards has
shrunk
down to a sad and scanty few.
My social obligations now
have thoroughly been weeded
through.

No wonder that my mantel
place
has lately looked so cold and
bare.
The folks who used to send me
cards
each year are just no longer
there.

A cautionary tale for me
remains in this outdated book:
I must have gratitude for life;
I'll be gone too at my next look.

Inertia

Sometimes I just don't want to
move,
but I'm not happy in that state.
I know that when I get things
done,
my lethargy evaporates.

Why do I need a big kick start
to make my stubborn engine
run?
God gave me coffee and a will.
"Get up," they say. "Work could
be fun."

"Yeah, right," I answer them so
glum.
My resistance is appalling.
But a flickering in my bad mood
shows me that work is calling.

And if I put one slow foot
gently in front of the other,
bit by bit, I increase my pace,
and my energy recovers.

Despedido

The river of life
is up to my neck,
and I've swum so far
I can't see the shore.

On out-going tide
I soon will be gone—
and will not return
to you anymore.

Goodbye. It's been nice,
but I've done my time.
I've tired, sad regrets,
but my love is yours.

Relationships and Feelings

A Mother's Prayer

Afghanistan, Iraq,
East Africa and back,
The Middle East, and
wherever we're attacked.
My soldier son has served
and come home without a
scratch.

In his familiar gym,
he gave his head a whack.
Blood and eighteen stitches,
and both his eyes were black.
He knocked himself out cold
and lay there on his back.

So, God, this is my prayer:
if you must, deploy him,
but keep his foolish ass
away from every gym.

Breaking Bad

*I always thought that I was
nice—
that I was sugar but not spice.
But someone crossed me
yesterday,
and you have never seen such
spite.*

*I always seek serenity,
so, what is going on with me?
I want to bite off people's heads
and spit them out, leave them
for dead.*

*From where does all this anger
rise?
Is it from years of telling lies—
from swearing that all things
are fine,
and if you hurt me, I don't
mind?*

I'm done with that, throw down
your gloves.
I finally see that it's not love
to let you get away with slights.
Throw down your gloves. We're
gonna fight.

It's not okay to step on me
however damaged you might be.
Not my problem; find your own
balm,
but don't expect me to stay calm.

I've had enough. My rage kicked
in,
and now you'll pay for every sin
both large and small, just as they
come,
until a new respect is won.

Possessed

Today my poem did not flow;
my fuzzy mind was very slow.
I fought demons all the night;
from dark to dawn, they would not go.

When I awoke and tried to rise,
my tangled sheets around me tied,
fell on the floor and bumped my head—
I guess I didn't beat those guys.

*I just can't stand to let them
win.
I'll scrabble for my trusty
pen,
and just when demons think
they've won,
I'll write a poem
denouncing them.*

Pushing Pigs Off the Porch

The pigs on my porch
keep coming back
though I sweep them off—
a big broom whacks.

They're tracking in mud,
and on my floor
piggy wallows form—
need to clean more.

One big and mean boar
turns and fights back.
The pig herder comes;
gives me some flack.

"My pigs always go
where they want to."
"But not on my porch!
Shoo! Shoo! Shoo! Shoo!"

I push on the boar;
he turns on me.
I'm 'bout to be gored
but I don't flee.

The herder jumps in
and grabs the boar
before I'm wounded
in this pig war.

He runs down the road
and shakes his fist.
He curses at me.
I get the gist.

The man loves his pigs.
They do no wrong,
and if I were kind,
I'd go along.

I wonder at that
and scratch my head.
When bound'ries are crossed,
give in instead?

Tug of War

You pull this way; I pull
that way.
Reinforcements line up
behind.
If I give in, will I resent
losing the war, changing my
mind?

Resentment is a deadly
draft
that murders love and rusts
the soul.
I can't afford to swallow it
if I want us to continue
whole.

*Someone has to relent with grace—
let go of my end of the rope,
choose to be happy if not right,
guard my relationship with hope.*

Seeking the Silver Lining

The soothing sun envelops me,
and from the bright blue
morning sky,
sweet breezes stroke my skin
with love,
but I'm so sad, I want to die.

Difficult choices burden me
with ugly options I don't like,
and any loathsome barb I choose
will shoot my worn-out heart a
spike.

I need to tweak my attitude
and seek to grasp a new insight.
I'm old enough to know by now
that where there's darkness,
there's still light.

Indecision

Nine o'clock in the morning
on January fifteenth,
I'm walking my weary laps
in the condo parking lot.
Tee-shirt weather has begun.
Bright sun warms my winter
skin.
A cool breeze refreshes me
when, at last, I feel too hot.

My husband offers his advice:
I should be in the cool pool.
Steadfast northern upbringing
Tells me, "Don't you be a fool.
You don't swim in wintertime."
My southern self chimes in with,
"Nothing foolish about it.
Now you're in another clime."

My last daily swim for the year
Was on November fifteenth—
the day my freezing was done.
Now, it's been two months at
least.
Maybe Florida winter
is finally on the run.
Maybe the pool is heating up.
At that, my reluctance ceased.

It's true nothing quite hydrates
my sun-dried Florida skin
like a reviving swim can.
Maybe early tomorrow,
I'll stick a trembling toe in.
I smile at the silly thought.
There now, I have a firm plan.

Praying Dog

When 'Genio and I
recite our morning prayers,
our Corgi mix is there.
He sits at my right side.

While I stand, he gazes
at the icon above.
His eyes fill up with love
while we sing God's praises.

Walking with Chico Suave

When I look for some exercise,
I take my dog outside.
But it should come as no
surprise,
he won't pick up his stride.

He stops at ev'ry tree and bush;
Our pace is like a snail,
and all because he's in no rush
to check on his p-mail.

Herding Butterflies

My dreams are butterflies I
chase
and each time I draw nigh,
they easily elude me
and flutter to the sky.

But once when I gave up, let
go,
and settled in repose,
a butterfly gently hovered
and landed on my nose.

Herding butterflies is futile,
to grasp at dreams is too,
but if you're calm and
patient,
they will come to you.

From the Poet's Mother

Note from the author:

Going through one of my mother's old albums, I found this poem in her handwriting, dated April 23, 1967:

Untitled
Cora Jean McKinney Cartmill Burnett

Lone and lost, my soul doth wander
   In and out through time and space
   Seeking for its own creator
   And a final homing place.

   Earth today but where tomorrow
   Shall my spirit find a home?
   Till at last, a happy harbor
   From whence ne'er again to roam.

   I shall enter and be welcomed.
   All my wanderings then shall cease.
   Found at last, my own creator
   In a realm of joy and peace.

*Thank you for reading this
collection.
The author welcomes your
feedback at
peginsula@aol.com*

www.ingramcontent.com/pod-product-compliance
Lightning Source LLC
Chambersburg PA
CBHW022229160726
47991CB00016B/2664